THE LITTLE HATMAKING BOOK

A WORKBOOK ON TURN-OF-THE-CENTURY HATS

Bonnie Holt Ambrose

Costume & Fashion Press
an imprint of
Quite Specific Media Group Ltd.
New York and Hollywood

© 1995 by Bonnie Holt Ambrose

All rights reserved under the International and Pan-American Copyright Conventions. For information address Quite Specific Media Group Ltd., 7373 Pyramid Place, Hollywood, CA 90046. Printed in Canada.

Email: info@quitespecificmedia.com

Voice: 323.851.5797
Fax: 323.851.5798

Quite Specific Media Group Ltd. imprints include:

Drama Publishers
Costume & Fashion Press
EntertainmentPro
By Design Press
Jade Rabbit

STEP 1

MAKE YOUR OWN BROWN PAPER PATTERN.
FOLLOW THE MEASUREMENTS BELOW.

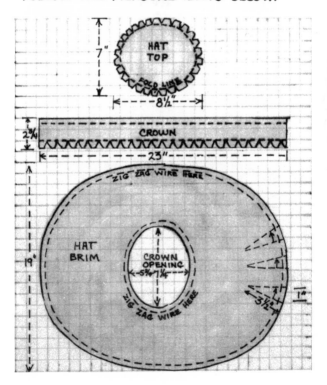

STEP 2

USING EXTRA HEAVY DOUBLE BUCKRAM, TRACE
AROUND PATTERN ONTO BUCKRAM WITH A
PENCIL. IT MAY BE NECESSARY TO PLACE
HEAVY OBJECTS AT CORNERS OF BUCKRAM.

USING A MEDIUM HEAT SETTING, IRON
BUCKRAM PIECES FLAT. CLIP NOTCHES
IN SEAMS WHERE INDICATED.

STEP 3

SET YOUR SEWING MACHINE STITCH TO THE
WIDEST AND LONGEST ZIG ZAG (APPROX: 4W X 6L)
OVERLAP ONE OF THE DART OPENINGS ON THE
HAT BRIM AND ZIG ZAG THE SEAM EDGES.
USE THE SAME METHOD ON THE OTHER
TWO DARTS.

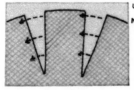

USE A
#16
NEEDLE

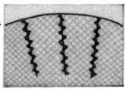

STEP 4

START AT CROWN OPENING AND CAREFULLY POSITION WIRE AT CENTER OF SEWING MACHINE FOOT. HAT WIRE SHOULD BE ½" FROM EDGE. SLOWLY ZIG ZAG WIRE TO CROWN OPENING. TO FINISH CIRCLE OF WIRE, LET ENDS OVERLAP AND TACK SECURELY, NOW ZIG ZAG WIRE ½" FROM OUTER EDGE OF HAT BRIM. USE CAUTION····YOU MAY BREAK NEEDLES. (USE #16 SEWING MACHINE NEEDLES.)

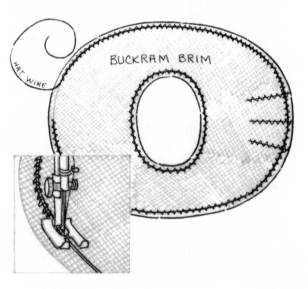

HAT WIRE

BUCKRAM BRIM

STEP 5

APPLY HAT WIRE WITH ZIG ZAG STITCH TO TOP EDGE OF BUCKRAM CROWN. SNIP EXCESS WIRE WITH WIRE CUTTERS.

SHAPE CROWN BAND INTO OVAL WITH WIRE TO THE INSIDE. COMPARE SIZE AND SHAPE WITH CROWN OPENING IN BRIM.

TACK STITCH CROWN BAND AT BACKSEAM.

BEND NOTCHED EDGES OUT ON CROWN AND DOWN ON HAT TOP.

HAT TOP SHOULD SLIDE INTO TOP OF CROWN (ALTERNATIVE METHOD: SET HAT TOP ONTO CROWN, BEND EDGES DOWN AND HOT GLUE.)

STEP 6

NOW YOU ARE READY TO HOT GLUE THE
HAT PIECES TOGETHER. CAFEFULLY
POSITION THE CROWN TO THE BRIM AND
HOT GLUE ONE FRONT TAB AND ONE
BACK TAB.

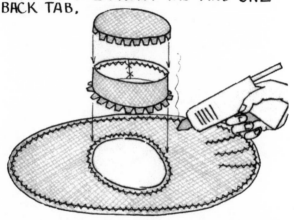

SLOWLY HOT GLUE YOUR WAY AROUND
ENTIRE CROWN. PATIENTLY FIT THE HAT
TOP INTO CROWN OPENING, TURN THE HAT
UPSIDE DOWN AND HOT GLUE TABS.
KEEP A BOWL OF ICE WATER NEAR IN
CASE OF HOT GLUE BURNS.

STEP 7

ONCE YOUR HAT FRAME IS COMPLETED, IT'S TIME TO CUT YOUR FABRIC COVERS. SELECT LIGHTWEIGHT FABRICS SUCH AS: SATIN, TAFFETA, LACE, SILK, POLY-SILK, CHIFFON, AND LIGHT BROCADES.

ENLARGE THE SIZE OF THE BROWN PAPER PATTERN BY ADDING 1" TO ALL THE SEAMS. CUT TWO FABRIC BRIM COVERS AND ONE HAT TOP COVER. USE A LIGHTER COLOR ON UNDER SIDE OF HAT BRIM TO LIGHTEN AND FRAME THE FACE.

SEW DARTS IN LOWER AND UPPER FABRIC BRIM COVERS. PRESS FLAT.

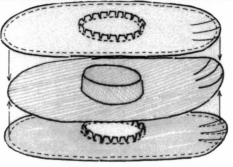

INSIDE OF FABRIC

STEP 8

POSITION TOP AND BOTTOM FABRIC TO
BUCKRAM FRAME, SO THAT ALL LAYERS
OF DARTS ARE MATCHING. FOLD BOTTOM
FABRIC UP OVER BRIM FRAME, USE TAPE
OR PINS TO SECURE. FOLD OUTSIDE SEAM
OF UPPER FABRIC TO THE INSIDE SO THAT
NO ROUGH EDGES ARE SHOWING.

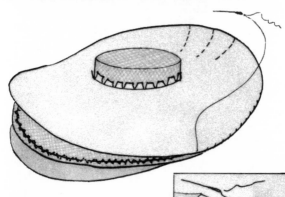

HAND-STITCH THE OUTER
EDGE SO THAT STITCHES
ARE ALMOST INVISIBLE.

FOLDED EDGES

STEP 9

POSITION FABRIC COVER FOR HAT TOP AND HOT GLUE TABS DOWN. CUT A 23" LENGTH OF 2" WIDE SATIN OR VELVET RIBBON, WRAP RIBBON AROUND CROWN AND TACK STITCH AT BACK SEAM.

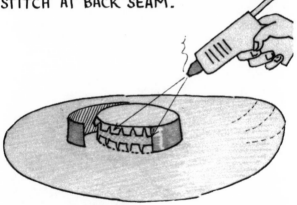

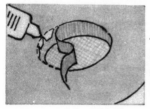

TURN HAT OVER AND HOT GLUE 1" BAND OF GROSGRAIN RIBBON INSIDE CROWN.

STEP 10

BELOW ARE SOME HINTS FOR
SECURING A LARGE BRIM HAT TO
THE HEAD.

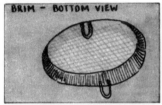

SMALL LOOPS ON
EACH SIDE OF THE
INSIDE HEADBAND
CAN BE USED WITH
BOBBIE PINS.

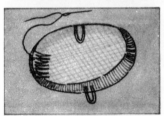

A SMALL COMB CAN
BE SEWN AT THE
FRONT OF THE
INSIDE HEADBAND.

CONNECT 1/4" WIDE
ELASTIC TO LOOPS.
SIZE THE ELASTIC
TO FIT UNDER HAIR
AT THE BACK OF
THE NECK.

DECORATING WITH TRIMS

VARIOUS STYLES CAN BE ACHIEVED BY
USING DIFFERENT FABRICS AND TRIMS,
AND THE MANNER IN WHICH THEY ARE
PLACED ON THE HAT.

BOW TRIM

FOR A LOVELY BOW, BUY 2¼ YARDS OF 3"
WIDE RIBBON AND FOLLOW THE DIRECTIONS
BELOW.

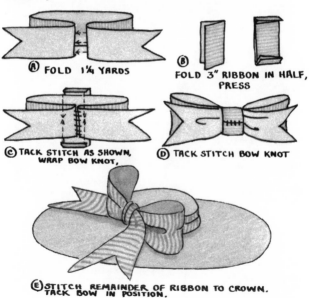

Ⓐ FOLD 1¼ YARDS

Ⓑ FOLD 3" RIBBON IN HALF,
PRESS

Ⓒ TACK STITCH AS SHOWN,
WRAP BOW KNOT.

Ⓓ TACK STITCH BOW KNOT

Ⓔ STITCH REMAINDER OF RIBBON TO CROWN.
TACK BOW IN POSITION.

EXTRA LARGE BOW

FOR A DRAMATIC OVER-SIZED BOW, CUT A
PAPER PATTERN FOLLOWING THE DIAGRAM
BELOW. USE A CRISP, OPAQUE FABRIC SUCH
AS TAFFETA. CUT TWO 1½ YARD LENGTHS OF
FABRIC AND ONE INNERFACING OF CRINOLINE
OR EXTRA HEAVY WEIGHT PELLON.

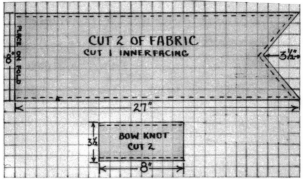

PLACE ON FOLD

8"

CUT 2 OF FABRIC
CUT 1 INNERFACING

3½"

27"

BOW KNOT
CUT 2

3½

8"

PLACE RIGHT SIDES OF FABRIC TOGETHER AND
BACK WITH CRINOLINE. SEW ALL THREE
PIECES OF FABRIC TOGETHER. LEAVE AN 8"
OPENING IN THE SEAM NEAR THE CENTER TO
ALLOW FOR TURNING.

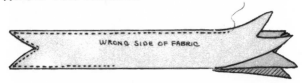

WRONG SIDE OF FABRIC

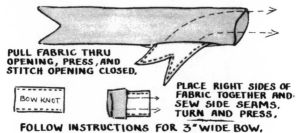

PULL FABRIC THRU
OPENING, PRESS, AND
STITCH OPENING CLOSED.

BOW KNOT

PLACE RIGHT SIDES OF
FABRIC TOGETHER AND
SEW SIDE SEAMS.
TURN AND PRESS.

FOLLOW INSTRUCTIONS FOR 3" WIDE BOW.

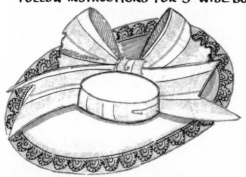

HAND SEW THE BOW IN POSITION AS REMOVAL
MAY BE NECESSARY LATER FOR PRESSING
OR RE-DECORATING.

THE LACE TRIM CAN BE ADDED BY BASTING
IT TO THE TOP FABRIC. SEW THE LACE 2"
FROM OUTSIDE EDGE.

TULLE AS TRIM

WITH ONE YARD OF TULLE MANY DIFFERENT
LOOKS CAN BE ACHIEVED. TULLE IS SOFT
AND LIGHTWEIGHT FOR MAKING BOWS,
RUFFLES, RUCHEING AND GATHERED HAT
LININGS.

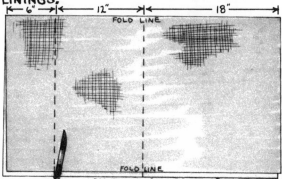

LAY TULLE OUT AS IT CAME OFF OF
THE BOLT. (WITH A DOUBLE FOLD)
CUT STRIPS AS SHOWN ABOVE.

USE THE 6" WIDE TULLE STRIP AND GATHER
IT ON BOTH EDGES. (BE SURE TO STITCH-1" IN
FROM EDGE) CAREFULLY PULL GATHERING
THREADS TO FORM A RUFFLE.

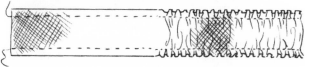

MEASURE OUTSIDE DIAMETER OF HAT. PREPARE
ENOUGH TULLE FOR A SLIGHTLY GATHERED
RUFFLE AT INSIDE EDGE OF HAT. PIN IN
POSITION. TIGHTEN UP INSIDE GATHERING
THREAD FOR A PERFECT
FIT. HAND-STITCH
BOTH GATHERED EDGES
TO UNDER FABRIC OF HAT.

FOLLOW DIRECTIONS
BELOW FOR TULLE
DECOR FOR HAT TOP.

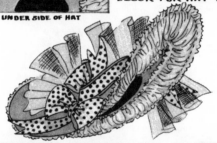

UNDER SIDE OF HAT

FOLD 18" TULLE IN HALF.
PRESS WITH WARM IRON.

GATHER ACROSS TULLE
EVERY 10".

PULL GATHERING
TIGHT AND TACK.

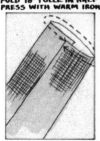

FEATHER TRIM

OSTRICH FEATHERS ARE A SOPHISTICATED LOOK FOR YOUR HAT. THEY BLEND WELL WITH TULLE AND RIBBON.

THE FOLLOWING IS A METHOD OF BENDING AND CURLING STRAIGHT OSTRICH PLUMES.

PRACTICE ON AN OLD FEATHER. YOUR IRON HEAT SETTING SHOULD BE MEDIUM-STEAM. LAY FEATHER WRONG SIDE UP.

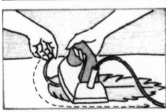

MOVE IRON FROM LARGEST PART OF QUILL, SLOWLY DOWN LENGTH OF FEATHER. WITH YOUR OTHER HAND CURL THE STEAMED PART OF THE FEATHER UP AND OVER THE IRON.

REPEAT THIS PROCEDURE UNTIL DESIRED EFFECT IS REACHED. HOLD CURL IN FEATHER WITH BOTH HANDS UNTIL COOL.

USE A THIN CURLING IRON
SET ON MEDIUM HEAT.
CURL 1½" WIDTHS OF
FEATHER AT A TIME.
BE SURE TO CURL FEATHER
TOWARD INSIDE OF QUILL.

TO ACHIEVE THE BOW PICTURED ON THE HAT
BELOW, FOLLOW THE INSTRUCTIONS FOR
THE EXTRA LARGE BOW. CHOOSE A 1½" WIDE
RIBBON OF CONTRASTING OR DARKER COLOR.
MACHINE STITCH DARKER RIBBON DOWN THE
CENTER OF THE EXTRA LARGE BOW.

DIFFERENT LOOKS — SAME TRIM

ROSE TRIM

FOLLOW MEASUREMENTS BELOW AND CUT A BROWN PAPER PATTERN, BE SURE TO PLACE PATTERN ON BIAS OF FABRIC, (BIAS: DIAGONALLY ACROSS GRAIN)

FOLD LINE — CUT 1 ON BIAS

SUGGESTED FABRICS — SILK ORGANZA, TAFFETA ORGANDY, SATIN, PEAU DE SOIE, OR FAILLE.

FOLD FABRIC DOWN CENTER AND PRESS, HANDSTITCH OR GATHER ON SEWING MACHINE. PULL GATHERING THREAD FOR LOOSE RUFFLE.

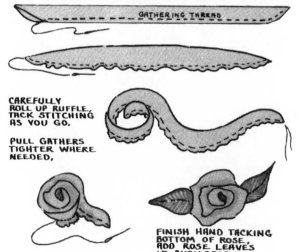

GATHERING THREAD

CAREFULLY ROLL UP RUFFLE, TACK STITCHING AS YOU GO.

PULL GATHERS TIGHTER WHERE NEEDED,

FINISH HAND TACKING BOTTOM OF ROSE, ADD ROSE LEAVES IF AVAILABLE.

THE SMALL BRIM HAT

THE SWEETHEART HAT IS A SIMPLE QUICK HAT THAT IS FLATTERING AND EASY TO WEAR.

STEP 1

START BY USING THE SAME METHOD
AS USED FOR THE WIDE BRIM HAT,
FOLLOW THE GRID BELOW TO MAKE
YOUR BROWN PAPER PATTERN.

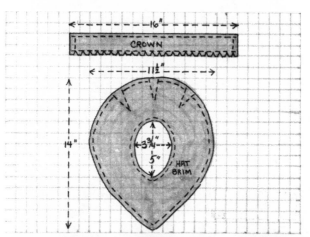

TRACE AROUND BROWN PAPER PATTERN.
ONE LAYER OF EXTRA HEAVY WEIGHT
BUCKRAM WILL WORK FOR THIS SMALL
HAT FRAME. A HAT TOP CAN BE USED
BUT IS NOT ESSENTIAL, ELIMINATING
THIS STEP WILL SAVE TIME.

FOLLOW INSTRUCTIONS GIVEN FOR THE WIDE BRIM HAT. OMIT CUTTING AND USING A HAT TOP PIECE. FOLLOW STEPS 2 THRU 6. THIS SMALL FRAME ONLY NEEDS ONE LAYER OF BUCKRAM AND NO HAT TOP, THEREFORE THE CONSTRUCTION TIME WILL BE SHORTER.

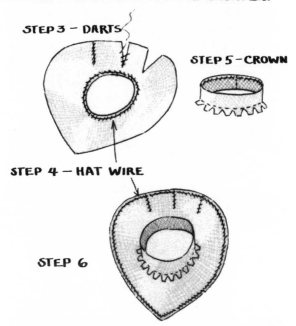

STEP 3 - DARTS

STEP 5 - CROWN

STEP 4 - HAT WIRE

STEP 6

SHEER BRIM COVER

AN EXCELLENT WAY TO SOFTEN THE LOOK OF YOUR HAT AND ADD DETAIL.

EXAMPLE: A SHEER LIGHT COLOR ORGANZA PLACED OVER A SATIN IN A DEEPER COLOR. TO ENHANCE THIS EFFECT FURTHER, GATHER THE SHEER ALONG THE INSIDE CROWN SEAM.
FOLLOW THIS GRID FOR YOUR PATTERN.

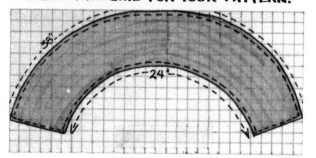

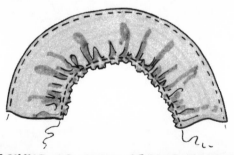

MACHINE OR HAND GATHER BOTH EDGES OF THE SHEER. TIGHTEN GATHERING THREAD TO FIT THE SIZE OF THE CROWN OPENING. STITCH THE ENDS TOGETHER.

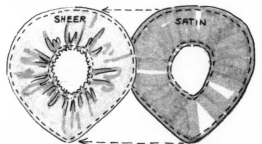

USE STRAIGHT PINS TO POSITION SHEER
COVER ON TO SATIN BRIM COVER.
MACHINE STITCH OUTER SEAM EDGES
TOGETHER. NOW STITCH INSIDE CROWN
SEAMS TOGETHER.

TURN TOP SATIN COVER Ⓑ FACE TO
FACE WITH SHEER Ⓒ AND UNDER SATIN
COVER Ⓐ. MACHINE STITCH TOGETHER,
LEAVING BACK HALF OF SEAM OPEN.

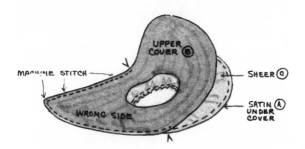

TRIM ¼" TO ½" FROM OUTSIDE EDGE
OF HAT FRAME. TURN COVER RIGHT SIDE
OUT AND PREPARE TO SLIDE HAT FRAME
INTO COVER.

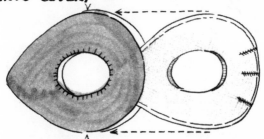

CLIP INSIDE SEAM OF THE CROWN
OPENING ⅜" (AS SHOWN ABOVE). THIS MAY
ALLOW THE HAT FRAME AN EASIER FIT.

TO CLOSE BACK BRIM SEAM, PIN
SMALL TUCKS WHERE EXTRA FULLNESS
OCCURS. WHIP STITCH SEAM CLOSED.

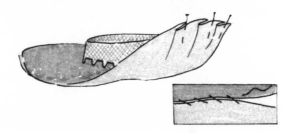

FOLLOW STEP 8 FOR INSTRUCTIONS ON
CLOSING OUTSIDE SEAM ON HAT BRIM.
HOT GLUE RIBBON AROUND CROWN AS
SHOWN IN STEP 9. USE LOOPS AND A
SMALL COMB TO SECURE THIS LIGHT
WEIGHT HAT ON THE HEAD

WIRE EDGE RIBBON
SHAPE AS SHOWN
TACK IN POSITION

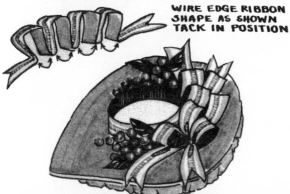

USE RIBBON WITH WIRE ALONG THE EDGES.
THIS RIBBON IS EASY TO STYLE AND
MAINTAINS IT'S SHAPE. WHEN DECORATING
YOUR HAT, HAND-SEWING THE TRIM PIECES
IN POSITION IS PREFERABLE. HOT
GLUE IS PERMANENT AND DOES NOT
ALLOW FOR EASY RE-TRIMMING LATER.

I hope this short guide to hatmaking has been helpful to you. Building period costumes & hats has captured my imagination & energy for the past Twenty-five years.   *Bonnie Holt-Ambrose*

MATERIALS: DOUBLE LAYER BUCKRAM, HATWIRE, CRINOLINE, HEAVY WEIGHT PELLON, BROWN PAPER,

TOOLS: SCISSORS, IRON, SEWING MACHINE #16 SEWING MACHINE NEEDLES, WIRE CUTTERS, HOT GLUE GUN, HOT GLUE STICKS, HAND SEWING NEEDLES, THREAD, STRAIGHT PINS, MASKING TAPE, CURLING IRON.

MATERIALS KIT AVAILABLE
TURN-OF-THE-CENTURY MATERIALS KIT INCLUDES: PATTERN, DOUBLE THICK BUCKRAM, AND HAT WIRE FOR MAKING ONE HAT.

FOR INFORMATION CALL OR WRITE TO ADDRESS ON BACK COVER.

ALSO AVAILABLE IN THIS SERIES:

THE LITTLE BODICE BOOK

A WORKBOOK ON BODICE CONSTRUCTION. A SIMPLE
GUIDE USING ONE BASIC BODICE PATTERN TO
ACHIEVE DIFFERENT STYLES AND PERIODS.

THE LITTLE CORSET BOOK

CORSET BUILDING MADE EASY. STEP-BY-STEP
INSTRUCTION FOR PRODUCING A DIFFICULT COSTUME
UNDERGARMENT.

SOON TO BE PUBLISHED:
THE LITTLE HATMAKING BOOK II

AN EASY TO FOLLOW GUIDE ON BUILDING ELIZABETHAN,
TUDOR AND RENAISSANCE HATS FOR MEN AND WOMEN.

ALSO AVAILABLE:

THE COSTUME WORKSHOP

A 'HOW-TO' TELEVISION SERIES DEMONSTRATING EASY
AND ECONOMICAL METHODS OF BUILDING COSTUMES.
THESE SHOWS ARE AVAILABLE IN 30 MINUTE V.H.S.

SHOW #1....LARGE BRIM VICTORIAN HAT FRAME
      CONSTRUCTION.
SHOW #2...COVERING AND TRIMMING A VICTORIAN
      HAT.
SHOW #3...FROM GARAGE SALE TO RENAISSANCE
      COSTUME.
SHOW #4...BUILDING A TURN-OF-THE-CENTURY CAPE
      AND SKIRT THE EASY WAY.
SHOW #5...FROM RESALE TO VICTORIAN WEDDING
      DRESS.
SHOW #6...AN "1830" UNIFORM COAT FROM A NAVY
      BLUE BLAZER.

SHOW #7...TRIMMING THE VICTORIAN WEDDING DRESS
       FROM SHOW 5.
SHOW #8...A SMALL BOY'S KNIGHT COSTUME THE
       EASY WAY.
SHOW #9...BUILDING LIGHT WEIGHT MEDIEVAL
       CROWNS.
SHOW #10..CONSTRUCTING AN INNVERNESS CAPE
       WITHOUT A PATTERN.

FOR A FREE BROCHURE AND FURTHER INFORMATION
CONTACT:

       BONNIE HOLT AMBROSE
       THE COSTUME WORKSHOP
       417 REINICKE
       HOUSTON, TEXAS 77007
       1 (713) 864-3969